A Big

Written by Emma Lynch

I will be the best.

Will jogs on the spot.

Rob flexes his legs.

Jan sits on a rug.

Will has a red vest.

Rob's vest is black.

Will and Rob run six laps.

Will wins.

Will and Rob get wet.

Rob swims best and wins.

Will and Rob pedal six laps.

Rob's legs spin ...

... but Will pedals best.

Rob gets a medal.

Will wins a cup.

Jan hops, skips and jumps!